DATE DUE			

Hodgkin's Disease

By Judith Peacock

Perspectives on Disease and Illness

LifeMatters
an imprint of Capstone Press
Mankato, Minnesota

Thank you to Bonnie Teschendorf, Director of Public Education at The Leukemia and Lymphoma Society.

LifeMatters books are published by Capstone Press
PO Box 669 • 151 Good Counsel Drive • Mankato, Minnesota 56002
http://www.capstone-press.com

Printed in the United States of America

Library of Congress Cataloging-in-Publication Data
Peacock, Judith, 1942–
    Hodgkin's disease / by Judith Peacock.
         p.   cm. — (Perspectives on disease and illness)
    Includes bibliographical references and index.
    ISBN 0-7368-1027-7
    1. Hodgkin's disease—Juvenile literature. [1. Hodgkin's disease. 2. Diseases.]
    I. Title. II. Series.
    RC644 .P43 2002
    616.99´446—dc21   00-012614
                                                                        CIP

    Summary: Discusses what Hodgkin's disease is and how it is diagnosed and managed; talks about coping with the disease; and takes a look at possible future treatments.

Staff Credits
Rebecca Aldridge, editor; Adam Lazar, designer; Kim Danger, photo researcher
Interior production by Stacey Field

Photo Credits
Cover: ©DigitalVision, left, right; ©Artville/Clair Alaska, middle; The Stock Market/©Howard Sochurek, bottom
©Artville/Clair Alaska, 37, 59
©DigitalVision, 27
Index Stock Imagery/©BSIP Agency, 9, 31; ©Richard Nowitz, 18
International Stock/©Patrick Ramsey, 42
Photo Network/©Bachmann, 17
©PhotoDisc/Barbara Penoyar, 49
Photri, Inc/15, 32, ©Tom Raymond, 28
Unicorn Stock Photos/©Jeff Greenberg, 41; ©Eric R. Berndt, 50
Uniphoto/Pictor/©Henryk T. Kaiser, 11
Visuals Unlimited/©E. Shelton-D. Fawcett, 6; ©Jeff Greenberg, 39; ©R. Calentine, 57

A 0 9 8 7 6 5 4 3 2 1

Table of Contents

1	What Is Hodgkin's Disease?	4
2	Diagnosing Hodgkin's Disease	12
3	Treatment for Hodgkin's Disease	22
4	Coping With Hodgkin's Disease	34
5	Brian's Story	44
6	Looking Ahead	52
	Glossary	60
	For More Information	61
	Useful Addresses and Internet Sites	62
	Index	63

Chapter Overview

Hodgkin's disease is a type of cancer known as a lymphoma. Lymphomas are cancers of the lymph system.

The lymph system produces, stores, and carries lymphocytes. These white blood cells help to protect the body against infection and disease.

Lymphomas are tumors that make the lymph nodes swell in size. These tumors can press on vital organs. Lymphomas also can lower a person's ability to resist disease and infection.

The two main types of lymphomas are Hodgkin's disease and non-Hodgkin's lymphomas. Hodgkin's disease differs from other lymphomas in cell type and the way it spreads.

No exact cause of Hodgkin's disease is known. It's possible that a virus such as the Epstein-Barr virus is associated with the development of Hodgkin's disease.

Hodgkin's disease tends to strike young adults ages 15 to 34 and older adults ages 55 to 70. More males than females get Hodgkin's disease. Certain risk factors may mean some people are more likely than others to get Hodgkin's disease. These factors include having a sibling with the disease, having had mononucleosis, and having a weak immune system.

Chapter 1

What Is Hodgkin's Disease?

"When my mother walked into my hospital room with the doctor, she looked **Naomi, Age 14** pale and shaken. I sensed that something was terribly wrong. The doctor sat on the side of the bed and put his hand on my arm. Then I knew that I was really, really sick. He said that I had Hodgkin's disease and that my body was full of tumors."

Hodgkin's disease is a type of cancer. It was named after Thomas Hodgkin, a British doctor. Dr. Hodgkin was the first person to describe the disease, which he did in 1832.

Hodgkin's disease belongs to a group of cancers known as lymphomas, which are cancers of the lymph system. That's why Hodgkin's disease also is called Hodgkin's lymphoma.

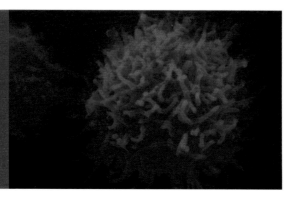

Lymphocytes are white blood cells that fight infection and disease.

The Lymph System

The lymph system is part of the body's immune system. It helps to provide the body with immunity, or protection, against infection and disease. It also cleanses body fluids and carries fat and other nutrients, or healthy substances, to parts of the body. Knowing about the lymph system is important for understanding Hodgkin's disease and other lymphomas.

Most people are familiar with the circulatory system, the system that circulates blood. The lymph system sometimes is called the body's "other circulatory system." That's because it, too, consists of a network of vessels, or tubes, that run throughout the body. Like blood vessels, lymphatic vessels branch into body tissues.

Instead of carrying blood, lymphatic vessels carry lymph, a colorless, watery fluid. Lymph contains lymphocytes, a type of white blood cell. When viruses and bacteria invade the body, lymphocytes produce substances called antibodies to fight them off.

Lymph nodes, or lymph glands, are other important parts of the lymph system. These small, bean-shaped organs are located along the network of lymph vessels. Clusters of lymph nodes can be found under the arms and in the neck, chest, abdomen, and groin. The groin is the hollow area that marks where the inner part of the thigh and pelvis meet. The pelvis is the lower part of the abdomen located between the hipbones. Lymph nodes make and store the germ-fighting white blood cells.

Other parts of the lymph system include the spleen and thymus. The spleen is an organ located near the stomach. The thymus is a gland located in the chest, behind the breastbone. The spleen and thymus also help to produce, store, and carry white blood cells. Bone marrow is considered part of the lymph system because it manufactures lymphocytes. Bone marrow is the soft, spongy tissue in the center of large bones. It's the source of immature cells for the lymphatic system and developing blood cells. The stomach, intestines, liver, and skin also contain lymphatic tissue.

Cancer of the Lymph System

Cancer is a disease of the body's cells. Normally, cells divide only to replace worn out or dying cells and to repair injuries. The process is controlled and orderly. Cancer cells are abnormal. They grow and divide uncontrollably. Cancer cells can cluster together and form a tumor, or a mass of cells. When tumors form a mass, they're called solid tumors.

More than 100 different kinds of cancer exist. The type of cancer depends on the part of the body where the abnormal cells first occur. Lymphoma is cancer that begins in lymphatic tissue. The ending *-oma* means "tumor," so lymphoma refers to tumors of the lymph system. Lymphoma can first appear almost anywhere in the lymph system.

There are four main types of Hodgkin's disease but at least 30 types of non-Hodgkin's lymphomas. Hodgkin's disease has a higher cure rate than non-Hodgkin's lymphomas. It often strikes young adults, while non-Hodgkin's lymphomas mainly affect older adults.

Hodgkin's Disease

Hodgkin's disease causes abnormal lymphocytes to multiply in the lymph nodes. The disease usually appears as swollen lymph nodes in the neck, under the arm, or in the groin. Like all cancers, Hodgkin's disease can metastasize, or spread, from its original site to other parts of the body. Abnormal cells leave the lymph nodes and pass into the bloodstream. They may travel to important body parts, especially the spleen, liver, lungs, bone, and bone marrow.

As mentioned earlier, abnormal cells can cluster together and form tumors. If they aren't stopped, tumors can grow large and press on organs, bones, and nerves. This pressure causes pain and interferes with the body's ability to function, which can lead to death. A person with advanced Hodgkin's disease also may die from an infection such as pneumonia. Too many abnormal white cells crowd out normal white cells and lower the person's ability to fight off germs.

Hodgkin's Disease Versus Non-Hodgkin's Lymphomas

About 15 percent of all lymphomas are Hodgkin's disease. The other 85 percent are called non-Hodgkin's lymphomas. Two main things set Hodgkin's disease apart from non-Hodgkin's lymphomas. For one thing, their cells have a different structure. Hodgkin's disease is characterized by unusually large cells called Reed-Sternberg (R-S) cells. R-S cells were named after the men who first identified them.

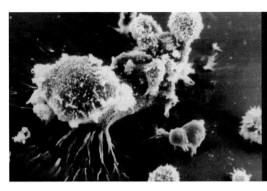

Cancer cells such as these can clump together to form tumors.

Another difference involves how the two lymphomas metastasize. Hodgkin's disease tends to spread in an orderly way. It usually goes from one lymph node to a neighboring node. Non-Hodgkin's lymphomas, on the other hand, often skip from one node group to another node group in a distant part of the body.

What Causes Hodgkin's Disease?

The exact cause or causes of Hodgkin's disease are not known. Some researchers believe that a virus may be linked to the development of Hodgkin's disease. Viruses can invade cells and cause them to become abnormal. One virus being studied is the Epstein-Barr virus, which causes mononucleosis and other infections. A number of people who have had mononucleosis later develop Hodgkin's disease.

Researchers do know that Hodgkin's disease isn't caused by an injury. A person's heredity doesn't seem to play a role, either. That means it doesn't seem to be passed down to people from their parents. In addition, Hodgkin's disease isn't contagious. It can't be spread from one person to another like a cold or the flu.

"My brother, Andy, was diagnosed with Hodgkin's disease when he was 21. He had just graduated from college. Andy wanted to be an airline pilot, but he never got a chance. He was too sick to work. It was awful to see him get so thin and weak. After four years of battling Hodgkin's, Andy died. I really miss him."

Jesse, Age 18

The rate of cancer among children and teens has been rising for decades. One reason may be exposure to new chemicals in the environment.

Who Gets Hodgkin's Disease?

More males than females develop Hodgkin's disease. The American Cancer Society estimated 7,400 new cases in the United States in 2000. Of these, 4,200 were expected to be male, and 3,200 were expected to be female. An equal number of males and females die from Hodgkin's disease each year. The American Cancer Society estimated 700 male and 700 female deaths in 2000.

Hodgkin's disease can occur in three different age groups. It can occur in people age 14 and younger but is rare in children younger than 5. People in early adulthood (ages 15 to 34) and late adulthood (ages 55 to 74) are more likely to have this disease. Hodgkin's disease affects Caucasians more often than African Americans.

Risk Factors for Hodgkin's Disease

Risk factors are things that increase a person's chances of developing a disease. People at risk for Hodgkin's disease may include the following:

A person whose brother or sister has had Hodgkin's disease.

People who have had mononucleosis.

People with reduced immunity, or ability to withstand disease. These might be people with AIDS or people who have had chemotherapy for cancer. They might be people who have had an organ transplant and take drugs that suppress the immune system. Some people are born with a faulty immune system.

Having a brother or sister who has had Hodgkin's disease increases a person's chance of developing the disease.

Having one or more of these risk factors doesn't mean that a person will get Hodgkin's disease. In fact, many people with Hodgkin's disease have no known risk factors.

Points to Consider

What do you think of when you hear the word *cancer?*

Do you know anyone with cancer? What is the disease like for that person?

How much did you know about Hodgkin's disease before reading this chapter? Do you know anyone with this illness?

Why might it be important to know about the risk factors for Hodgkin's disease or any other disease?

Chapter Overview

The most common early symptom of Hodgkin's disease is a painless swelling of lymph nodes. Other symptoms include fever, night sweats, weight loss, itching, and fatigue. Several other diseases and infections have the same symptoms.

A physical examination by a doctor, blood tests, and imaging tests are important for diagnosing Hodgkin's disease.

A biopsy of the lymph nodes is the most important step in diagnosing Hodgkin's disease. A biopsy shows whether or not a person's tissue contains R-S cells.

Following a diagnosis of Hodgkin's disease, the illness is typed and staged. Typing is figuring out what kind of Hodgkin's the person has. Staging means determining how far the cancer has spread.

Chapter 2

Diagnosing Hodgkin's Disease

Early diagnosis, or detection, of Hodgkin's disease can be difficult. Many people in the beginning stages of this illness have no symptoms, so they don't seek medical attention. Still others have symptoms that are similar to other diseases and infections such as mononucleosis or tuberculosis. Doctors may misdiagnose these people and treat them for the wrong condition.

Signs and Symptoms of Hodgkin's Disease

The most common early symptom of Hodgkin's disease is a lump that doesn't go away. Such a lump especially in the neck, armpit, or groin is a sign. The lump is a lymph gland that has become enlarged because of too many lymphocytes. The swelling usually is painless, so many people with early Hodgkin's disease ignore the lump.

"If you feel a lump in your neck or anywhere else on your body, get it checked out right away. Don't wait until you feel pain. Hodgkin's disease may not cause pain early on."—Brenda, age 15

Other early signs and symptoms of Hodgkin's disease include the following:

Unexplained fever that comes and goes for several days or weeks

Night sweats (heavy sweating in bed during the night)

Weight loss

Severe itching

Ongoing fatigue, or constant tiredness

As the disease progresses, the person may feel back and leg pain. He or she may cough a lot and be short of breath. There may be weight loss, nausea, and vomiting. Nausea is an upset stomach. Vomiting is throwing up. Tumors that press on organs, nerves, and bones usually cause these symptoms.

Steps in Diagnosis

Steps in diagnosing Hodgkin's disease include a review of the person's medical history and a physical examination. Medical tests and a biopsy also are needed for diagnosis.

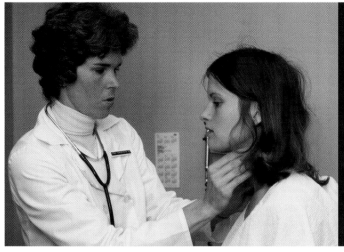

Part of a physical exam for Hodgkin's disease includes checking the lymph nodes.

Medical History

Knowing a person's medical history and general health is important for a beginning diagnosis. A doctor finds out a person's medical history by asking questions about the person's symptoms. The doctor asks about the person's history of disease and illness, as well as his or her family's. A person's age can be important, too. For example, it's normal for children to have larger lymph nodes than adults have.

Physical Examination

Diagnosing Hodgkin's disease begins with a physical examination. The person may go to the doctor because of swollen glands or other symptoms. Sometimes, however, the doctor discovers an enlarged lymph node during a routine checkup or X ray. The doctor notes the size, location, tenderness, and firmness of the lymph node. He or she checks to see if other areas of the body are involved.

Most lymph node enlargement is the result of an infection, not Hodgkin's disease. If the doctor thinks the cause is an infection, he or she probably will prescribe an antibiotic. This medicine kills bacteria and fights infection. The glands may not return to normal size within a few weeks. Or, the doctor may suspect something more serious. In either case, the doctor will probably order various medical tests.

At a Glance

The symptoms of mononucleosis include swollen glands, chills, fever, sore throat, and fatigue. The disease doesn't cause death. Most people get well in three to six weeks.

> "I remember the summer I was diagnosed with Hodgkin's disease. I was **Jacob, Age 17** doing a lot of swimming and hiking and having a really great time. Then the fevers started. Sometimes they'd get up to 102 degrees. I was having night sweats, and my skin was really itchy. I couldn't sleep, and my stress level was so high that I'd jump when the phone rang. I went to the community health clinic and got some antibiotics, but they didn't help."

Medical Tests

Blood tests and imaging tests can provide more information about the person's condition. Blood tests can detect signs of disease. In some cases, they also can diagnose specific diseases. For example, mononucleosis can be identified by the presence of certain antibodies. Although no blood test is available for Hodgkin's disease, blood tests can rule out other diseases. This narrows the choices for diagnosis.

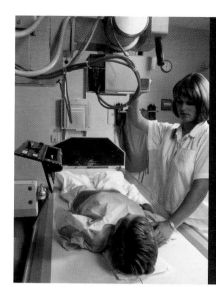

An X ray is one medical test that can help determine whether a person has Hodgkin's disease.

Imaging tests are pictures of the body's insides. They often can show the location and size of tumors. Imaging tests for Hodgkin's disease include the following:

X rays of the chest, bones, liver, or spleen. High-energy radiation is used to take pictures. An enlarged spleen can be another sign of Hodgkin's disease.

Computed tomography (CT) scan of the abdomen. A computer linked to an X-ray machine creates a series of pictures taken from many angles. These are combined to form one complete picture. A CT scan can show enlarged lymph nodes that may be deep in the abdominal cavity.

Magnetic resonance imaging (MRI). Radio waves and a powerful magnet linked to a computer produce detailed pictures. These pictures show soft tissue changes.

Biopsy

A final diagnosis of Hodgkin's disease depends on the results of a biopsy. A biopsy, also called a tissue biopsy, is the examination of living tissue under a microscope. It proves whether the person has Hodgkin's disease.

A pathologist uses a microscope to examine the tissue or fluid from a biopsy.

A tissue sample can be removed from a person in two main ways.

Surgical biopsy. This involves cutting out an entire lymph node or a small part of a large tumor. The tumor may be deep inside the chest or abdomen. If so, the biopsy is done in a hospital operating room, and the person is put to sleep. If the tumor is near the skin's surface, the person usually is given medicine to numb the area. Then the tumor is removed.

Fine needle aspiration biopsy. Doctors draw out a small amount of fluid and tiny bits of tissue from the tumor. This involves using a thin needle and syringe, or tube with a plunger.

A pathologist in a laboratory examines the tissue or fluid after removal. A pathologist is a doctor who studies tissue for signs of disease. Using a microscope, the pathologist looks for the cells that identify Hodgkin's disease, especially R-S cells. The presence of these cells usually means that the person has Hodgkin's disease.

Screening tests are available to detect specific cancers before symptoms become apparent. For example, a mammogram is a special X ray that can detect breast cancer. Unfortunately, no screening test exists for Hodgkin's disease.

Types of Hodgkin's Disease

The pathologist also tries to determine the type of Hodgkin's disease the person has. Knowing the type is important for planning treatment. A fast-growing type needs quicker, stronger treatment than a slower-growing type does. There are four types of Hodgkin's disease.

Nodular sclerosis is the most common type. About 30 to 60 percent of Hodgkin's disease cases are nodular sclerosis.

Lymphocyte predominant is the slowest-growing type. It accounts for 5 to 10 percent of cases.

Lymphocyte depleted is the fastest-growing type. However, it accounts for less than 5 percent of cases.

Mixed cellularity makes up about 20 to 40 percent of Hodgkin's disease cases.

Staging Hodgkin's Disease

Following diagnosis, the person's Hodgkin's disease is staged. Staging means determining how far the cancer has spread. It also involves predicting where the cancer might spread in the future. Staging is very important for planning treatment.

Fast Fact Each year in the United States, cancer is diagnosed in an estimated 8,000 children younger than age 15. Acute lymphoblastic leukemia and brain cancer are the most common forms of cancer diagnosed in children and teens.

Stages of Hodgkin's Disease

There are four stages of Hodgkin's disease.

Stage 1. The cancer is still within one lymph node area.

Stage 2. The cancer involves two or more lymph node areas. However, they are either all above or all below the diaphragm. This is the thin layer of muscle below the heart and lungs that separates the chest from the abdomen.

Stage 3. The cancer involves lymph node areas both above and below the diaphragm. It also may have spread to the spleen.

Stage 4. The cancer has spread to one or more organs outside the lymph system, such as the liver.

These stages are further divided into categories A and B. People in category A have no symptoms. People who do have symptoms such as night sweats are in category B.

How Hodgkin's Disease Is Staged

Staging Hodgkin's disease requires many of the same tests that diagnosing the disease does. In addition to X rays, CT scans, and MRIs, doctors may use gallium scans. In this test, a radioactive substance called gallium shows the size and location of tumors or enlarged lymph nodes.

Doctors may perform additional biopsies to determine staging. For example, they may use fine needle aspiration to biopsy bone marrow.

> "I went to see my doctor about a backache. When I mentioned that I felt some tightness when breathing, my doctor ordered a chest X ray.
>
> **Maren, Age 16**
>
> "The next morning I went back to the doctor. He pulled out the X ray and pointed to a dark mass on it. 'See this? It's not supposed to be there,' he said.
>
> "I was admitted to the hospital for a biopsy operation. I woke up in intensive care. The doctors had opened up my whole chest to get at the tumors. I was in stage 3 of Hodgkin's disease."

Points to Consider

Have you or someone in your family ever been diagnosed with a serious illness? If yes, how did you react? If no, how do you think you would react?

How might a diagnosis of Hodgkin's disease change your life?

Why might a person's medical history be important in diagnosing Hodgkin's disease?

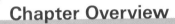

Chapter Overview

Standard treatment for Hodgkin's disease consists of radiation therapy, chemotherapy, or a combination of both.

Radiation therapy uses high-energy waves to destroy cancer cells or slow their growth. It may involve one or more areas of the body. Chemotherapy uses strong drugs to destroy cancer cells throughout the body or to shrink tumors.

Treatment for Hodgkin's disease has risks and benefits. On the one hand, it's very successful in the early stages of the disease. On the other hand, it can produce long-term and late side effects.

Doctors might recommend a bone marrow transplant for people whose Hodgkin's disease resists standard treatment. They also may recommend it for people whose cancer comes back.

Complementary therapy goes along with and supports standard treatment. Alternative therapy takes the place of standard treatment but may be harmful to a person.

Chapter 3

Treatment for Hodgkin's Disease

Standard treatment for Hodgkin's disease consists of radiation therapy, chemotherapy, or a combination of both. The exact treatment depends on the disease's type and staging and the size of the tumors. It also depends on the person's symptoms, age, and general health.

Radiation Therapy

Radiation therapy, or radiotherapy, uses X-ray waves to destroy cancer cells or slow their growth. It can be used to shrink tumors, too. Radiation therapy doesn't cause the body to become radioactive. It treats the tumor and a small amount of surrounding tissue. It generally is used for stages 1 and 2 of Hodgkin's disease. It's also used to relieve pain.

Surgery is used for biopsy and staging Hodgkin's disease. It isn't used to treat the illness.

How External Beam Radiation Therapy Is Done

Radiation therapy for Hodgkin's disease usually is given externally, or on the outside of the body. Prior to the first treatment, the radiologist and other specialists plan exactly how the treatment will be done. They use computers, imaging devices, and other equipment to assist their planning.

During treatment, the person lies very still on a cushioned table. A radiation therapy machine aims a beam of high-energy rays toward the target area. The dosage is calculated as accurately as possible to reduce side effects. Special markings on the person's body help direct the beam to the exact site. Lead blocks or shields further protect nontarget areas of the body from radiation. Padding and other devices keep the person's body in the right position.

Setting up the person for each treatment may take from 15 to 30 minutes. The treatment itself may take less than one minute. External beam radiation usually is given daily, Monday through Friday. Daily therapy gives cancer cells less time to multiply. The therapy goes on for three to six months with rest periods. The person generally goes to a hospital radiology department for treatment.

"At the beginning of radiation, the technician marked my skin with semipermanent ink. She drew tiny, freckle-sized dots around the area for radiation. My chest looked like one of those connect-the-dot drawings I used to do as a kid."—Tina, age 15

"Radiation wasn't so bad. I still was able to go to school half days. I only had to have 30 treatments, which isn't bad considering that some people have a lot more. Toward the end, though, it was really getting to be a drag. I got really tired of the routine."

Jared, Age 16

Short-Term Side Effects of External Beam Radiation Therapy
Although radiation therapy doesn't hurt, it can cause unpleasant side effects. The person may feel tired and lack energy. The skin in the target area may become red, dry, tender, and itchy. Radiation may need to be given to the chest or neck. This can cause a dry, sore throat, trouble swallowing, shortness of breath, and a dry cough.

Radiation given to the abdomen may cause nausea, vomiting, diarrhea, and urinary problems. Diarrhea is a condition in which normally solid waste becomes runny and frequent. People with urinary problems have trouble ridding the body of its liquid waste. Fortunately, these side effects usually go away once treatment stops.

Hodgkin's disease was one of the first cancers to be cured with chemotherapy.

Radiation Therapy in Children and Teens With Hodgkin's Disease

Children and teens who haven't reached their full growth generally receive only low doses of radiation. That's because radiation affects bone and muscle growth. Large doses of radiation can prevent children from reaching their normal size. Other growth problems such as unusually small teeth can result as well. Children and teens with Hodgkin's disease often begin their treatment with chemotherapy rather than radiation therapy.

Chemotherapy

Chemotherapy uses strong drugs to destroy cancer cells and shrink tumors. Oncologists, or doctors who treat cancer, usually prescribe a mixture of drugs. Different drugs kill cancer cells in different ways and thus increase the chances of success. Rather than treating one area, the drugs enter the bloodstream and travel throughout the body. Chemotherapy often is the first method of treatment for stages 3 and 4 of Hodgkin's disease.

How Chemotherapy Is Done

Chemotherapy may be given by mouth in pill or liquid form. Usually, however, it's given by intravenous (IV) infusion in a hospital outpatient clinic or doctor's office. The person may sit in a big chair while receiving the drugs through a needle. Other people receiving chemotherapy may be in the room as well. A nurse inserts a tiny tube into a vein in the person's forearm. The tube is connected to a bag containing the drug mixture. The drugs slowly drip from the bag through the tube and into the person's bloodstream.

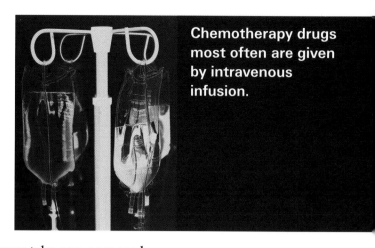

Chemotherapy drugs most often are given by intravenous infusion.

A session of chemotherapy may take one or more hours. Chemotherapy generally is given in courses or cycles. The person goes through a treatment period followed by a rest period. Then, he or she has a treatment period again, and so on. Regular blood tests determine whether the person has a healthy number of red and white blood cells and platelets. Platelets help blood to clot. A person needs enough cells and platelets to be able to continue treatment. Chemotherapy may last from nine months to a year, depending on the person's response during the first six months.

Short-Term Side Effects of Chemotherapy

Chemotherapy is well known for its difficult side effects. Short-term side effects can include hair loss, poor appetite, nausea, vomiting, and mouth sores. A person on chemotherapy is likely to get infections, bruise or bleed easily, and feel weak and tired. Side effects occur because chemotherapy kills rapidly dividing cells. Cancer cells divide rapidly, but so do some healthy cells. Some healthy cells that divide rapidly include those in hair roots, the digestive tract, and the blood.

Side effects of chemotherapy vary depending on specific drugs and dosages. They also vary with the person being treated. Not everyone reacts to drugs in the same way. Some people have few or no side effects. In addition, medications and treatments are available to help reduce nausea, discomfort, or fatigue.

A possible side effect of chemotherapy is having hair fall out. Hair grows back once chemotherapy treatments are done.

"When I started chemotherapy, I knew my hair might fall out. I just didn't know how or when it would happen.

Reine, Age 15

"My friend Tessa invited me to her house for a sleepover. We took turns doing each other's hair. I combed and styled Tessa's hair, which was long and thick like mine.

"When it was my turn, Tessa asked me how I wanted my hair fixed. I said I wanted a French braid. I knew something was wrong with the first stroke of the comb. I could feel Tessa become tense. She put the comb through again, and then she gasped.

"I turned around and saw the comb. It held a huge hunk of my hair. I screamed in horror. Even though I had expected to lose my hair, I still wasn't prepared. I was so upset that I had to call my mom to come and get me."

"When I had chemo, I felt like I had the flu all the time. Some days were worse than others. I told myself that I was going to make it. I would just take one day at a time and see what I could do."—Terrell, age 17

Good News, Bad News

Hodgkin's disease is one of the most treatable forms of cancer. That's the good news. The bad news is that radiation therapy and chemotherapy can result in serious long-term side effects and late effects. People with Hodgkin's disease need to understand the benefits and risks of treatment.

A Highly Curable Cancer

Most people with Hodgkin's disease can be cured, or their disease can be controlled for many years. By "cured," doctors generally mean that the person shows no signs of the disease five or more years after treatment. Instead of *cured*, some doctors prefer to use the word *remission*. Remission means that the cancer is gone for now but that it can return. People who are diagnosed and treated in the early stages of Hodgkin's disease have a good chance of surviving. They have a good chance of living a normal life span.

Fast Fact

According to the American Cancer Society, 82 percent of people with Hodgkin's disease survive at least five years after diagnosis.

Long-Term Side Effects and Late Effects

Radiation therapy and chemotherapy can save lives, but they also can have long-term side effects. For example, radiation therapy may need to be done to the testes or ovaries. These are parts of the male and female reproductive system. Radiation therapy to these areas can result in temporary or permanent fertility loss. Fertility means the ability to have children. Some children who receive radiation to the brain develop learning problems. Chemotherapy may damage the immune system, which makes a person more susceptible to serious infections.

Radiation therapy and chemotherapy also can have late effects. The term *late effects* refers to new illnesses or conditions that develop months, even years, after treatment. A serious late effect for people with Hodgkin's disease is a second cancer. For example, a young woman may receive radiation therapy to treat lymphoma in her chest. This woman may develop breast cancer in later years. Leukemia, lung cancer, and thyroid cancer are sometimes found among people who have been treated for Hodgkin's disease. The thyroid is a gland located in the front of the neck.

Radiation therapy to the head and neck can cause hypothyroidism in some people. This means their thyroid gland slows down. The result can be weight gain, lack of energy, constipation, and feeling cold. Constipation means having trouble ridding the body of its solid waste.

Acupuncture is a complementary therapy that may relieve pain, nausea, and vomiting caused by chemotherapy.

Bone Marrow Transplants

Some people with Hodgkin's disease become resistant to standard treatment. Standard radiation and chemotherapy no longer destroy or slow their cancer. Other people who have been treated successfully for Hodgkin's disease may have a recurrence. They were in remission, but their cancer comes back. In these cases, doctors may try a bone marrow transplant.

Bone marrow transplants, which are relatively new, help restore the production of blood cells. A supply of healthy blood cells allows people with Hodgkin's disease to have higher doses of chemotherapy and radiation. Chapter 6 describes bone marrow transplants in more detail.

Complementary and Alternative Therapies

Two other kinds of therapy are complementary therapy and alternative therapy. Complementary therapy goes along with and supports standard treatment. It may help to relieve pain, reduce side effects, or improve the person's overall well-being. Examples of complementary therapy include acupuncture, biofeedback, and stress management. Acupuncture is a Chinese practice that involves placing needles on the body. This can relieve the pain, nausea, and vomiting that chemotherapy causes. Biofeedback is a technique for controlling body functions such as heartbeat. Prescription drugs to stimulate the appetite or relieve itching are another kind of complementary therapy.

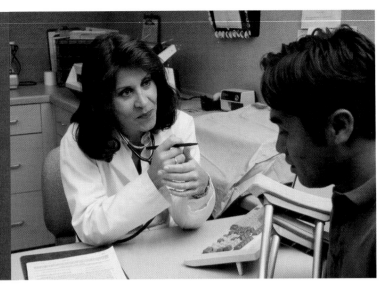

It's important to talk with your doctor before beginning any complementary or alternative therapy.

Alternative therapy takes the place of standard treatment. Unlike standard treatment, alternative therapy hasn't been scientifically proven to destroy or slow down cancer. Alternative therapy examples include taking huge doses of vitamins, drinking herbal teas, or relying on prayer or positive thinking. Taking drugs that haven't been approved by the government is another kind of alternative therapy. People may turn to alternative therapy because of religious or personal beliefs or because standard treatment hasn't been successful.

People with Hodgkin's disease should consult a medical doctor before choosing alternative and complementary therapies. Alternative therapies may help a person by offering hope, but they can be dangerous. A person with Hodgkin's disease also can lose valuable treatment time by following an alternative therapy. While complementary therapies generally are effective, some may not be safe for some people.

Points to Consider

What do you think it might be like to go through radiation therapy or chemotherapy? Do you know anyone who has had radiation therapy or chemotherapy? What was the experience like for that person?

Would you undergo treatment for Hodgkin's disease if you knew you might develop a second cancer later? Why or why not?

Why would not smoking be especially important for a person who has been treated for Hodgkin's disease?

How could you help a friend or family member cope with treatment for Hodgkin's disease?

What do you think would be the biggest challenge of receiving treatment for Hodgkin's disease?

Chapter Overview

Hodgkin's disease affects not only the person who is ill but also his or her family and friends. It can turn everyone's life upside down.

Health care professionals can help a person with Hodgkin's disease cope with the side effects of treatment. They also can help the person deal with the fear, worry, and anger that often go with being ill.

Brothers and sisters of a teen with Hodgkin's disease also may struggle with difficult emotions. They can learn to act in ways that help themselves and their sibling.

Friends of a teen with Hodgkin's disease can help by staying in touch and listening. Doing things together can help take the teen's mind off being sick.

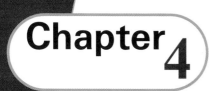

Chapter 4

Coping With Hodgkin's Disease

A serious illness such as Hodgkin's disease can disrupt a person's whole life. It can make his or her future uncertain. The experience can be very frightening and lonely. Coping with Hodgkin's disease can be difficult for the person who is ill. It also can be hard on everyone involved in his or her life.

Coping With Hair Loss

- Before starting chemotherapy, get a short, stylish haircut. This can help prepare you for the change in the way you look. It also cuts down on the amount of hair that falls out. If you really want to feel in control, shave your head.

- Once treatment has started, handle your hair gently. Wash it with a mild soap, pat it dry, and carefully comb through it. If you use a hairdryer or curling iron, put it on low heat. Avoid hair dyes and permanent waving lotions.

- If all your hair has fallen out, wear a hat, scarf, or wig, or go bald. Hold your head high and imagine that you're part of the latest fashion trend.

- If you plan to wear a wig, buy it before you begin losing your hair. You'll have an easier time matching your hair color and style.

If You Have Hodgkin's Disease

"My Hodgkin's disease has turned out to be trickier and more complicated than most cases. The doctors thought that six weeks of radiation therapy would cure me, but it didn't. I recently finished six months of chemotherapy, and the outcome still is uncertain.

Luke, Age 17

"My friends have been great. They include me in their activities, and I can keep up pretty well. When they start talking about college and their plans for the future, though, I feel left out. I don't know what my future will be or if I'll even have one."

A history of exercise is one example of a personal strength that may help you get through treatment.

If you're a teen with Hodgkin's disease, no one needs to tell you how difficult things can be. You must deal not only with physical pain but also with emotional distress. Be assured that many trained and skilled people are available to help you. These people include your primary physician, oncologist, oncology nurses, and radiation oncologist. A nutrition counselor, social worker, and mental health counselor also can be part of your cancer care team. Work with these professionals to promote your physical and emotional well-being.

When you're in treatment, make a list of questions to ask your oncologist and other health care professionals. Find out about side effects and what you can do to make them less troublesome. Identify your special strengths or things that will help you do better in treatment. For example, maybe you have a strong family support system or a history of good nutrition and exercise. Some people with cancer find that a deep, spiritual faith calms their fear of treatment.

Did You Know?

"Cell-Mates" is a one-to-one support program sponsored by the Lymphoma Research Foundation of America. People who have survived lymphoma volunteer to share their experience with others who are coping with this disease. Cell-Mates communicate either over the phone, by e-mail, or through letters.

After treatment, be sure to have regular physical exams, blood tests, and imaging studies. Keep flu shots and other vaccinations up-to-date and treat all infections carefully. Follow-up care can help you guard against long-term and late effects of radiation and chemotherapy. Teen women who have been treated for Hodgkin's disease should have regular mammograms to detect breast cancer. Other important aspects of follow-up care include managing stress, eating a nutritious diet, exercising, and not smoking. Your cancer care team can help you plan a healthy lifestyle.

Belonging to a support group during and after treatment is a great way to cope with Hodgkin's disease. Support groups consist of people who have had similar problems and experiences. They can provide emotional support, friendship, and understanding. Support groups for teens with cancer are available in many communities. Check the back of this book for help finding a group near you.

You may have to take on more responsibilities at home if your brother or sister has Hodgkin's disease.

If Your Brother or Sister Has Hodgkin's Disease

If you have a brother or sister with Hodgkin's disease, your life will be affected, too. Your parent or parents may be taking your sibling to treatment, which can make family life more hectic. Hospital and doctor bills may force the family to cut back on expenses. That may mean less money for you to spend on clothes and entertainment. You may be expected to take on more responsibility at home. Your parent or parents may not be able to give you the attention you need.

You may experience a variety of upsetting feelings as a result of your sibling's illness. You may worry whether your brother or sister will get well. At the same time, you may feel jealous because your sibling is getting so much attention. Anger and resentment may surface if you must give up your plans or go without things you want. You may feel guilty about feeling good when your brother or sister feels terrible. All these feelings are natural.

You might try these suggestions for coping with your brother or sister's illness.

Try to live as normally as possible. Stick to your daily routine and continue to participate in your usual activities. Doing familiar things can help you feel more secure during difficult times.

Find out more about Hodgkin's disease and its treatment. For example, do you know how chemotherapy and radiation are given? Knowing more about the illness will help you understand what your brother or sister is going through. If you're concerned about your chances of developing Hodgkin's disease, talk with your sibling's doctor.

Let your brother or sister know you haven't forgotten about him or her. Leave notes and homemade cards for your sibling to read. If possible, participate in your brother or sister's treatment in some way. For example, you might obtain tapes he or she can listen to during chemotherapy. You probably will feel closer to your sibling if you can help out.

Let out your feelings in a healthy way. You might talk with a parent, school counselor, coach, teacher, or spiritual advisor. You might write in a journal. Allowing anger, guilt, and worry to build up inside can harm your physical and emotional health.

Remember that your parents still love you, even though they may be busy caring for your sibling. If you were the one who was sick, they would care for you the same way.

Spending time doing regular family activities may help a family cope when a member has Hodgkin's disease.

If Your Friend Has Hodgkin's Disease

"Amy and I have been best friends for six years. After Amy started chemo for Hodgkin's disease, I felt uncomfortable around her. It was hard to see her lose her hair and all. I didn't talk to her for a long time. Then I realized that I had to stop being so selfish and quit focusing on how upset I was. I needed to think about Amy.

Laneesha, Age 14

"One Friday night, I showed up at her house with a stack of videos. We watched movies all night. Actually, we did more talking than watching. We had a lot to catch up on. After that, I went over to her house a lot, especially after a chemo session. I knew she needed something to help take her mind off being sick.

"Amy's six months of chemotherapy are finished now, and she's in remission. I think that if we made it through all this, we'll probably be best friends forever."

Doing fun activities together is one way to help a friend who has Hodgkin's disease.

Most teens lack experience in supporting someone with a serious illness. They may think they don't know what to say or do. As a result, they may stay away from that person, even if that person is a friend. But a friend who is ill needs your attention more than ever. If you have a friend with Hodgkin's disease, you might follow these suggestions.

Try not to let the person's appearance scare you off. Even if your friend looks different, he or she is the same person inside.

Before visiting, check with your friend's family to see if your friend can have visitors. If your friend's white blood cell count is low, he or she might risk infection by having visitors. You may have to limit yourself to phone calls.

Be willing to listen. Don't worry about what to say. Don't think you have to offer advice or solve problems. Just letting your friend talk about his or her feelings is enough.

Keep your friend up-to-date on what's happening at school. Bring or send him or her copies of the school newspaper. You might make a videotape or an audiotape of messages from classmates.

"I used the Internet to find out a lot of practical information about Hodgkin's disease. For example, I learned some ways to cope with side effects. I also found some places to buy wigs and scarves. When my urine turned dark red, I wasn't scared. I knew from the Internet that this was a side effect of one of the chemo drugs I was taking."—Tracy, age 17

Advice
From Teens

Help your friend keep current with schoolwork. You might bring books and assignments from school, tape-record lectures and class discussions, and take notes.

Think of things to do that will amuse your friend and help pass the time.

Points to Consider

Has anyone in your family ever been seriously ill or injured? What things did you do as a family to cope?

Imagine your best friend has Hodgkin's disease. How do you think you'd react? What could you do to help your friend?

What do you think are some good ways to cope with having a serious illness?

Chapter Overview

People with Hodgkin's disease face many difficult emotions including anger, fear, and guilt. Dealing with these emotions is an important part of becoming healthy again.

Because the causes of Hodgkin's disease are unknown, there is no known way to prevent it. People with Hodgkin's disease shouldn't feel guilty about having this illness.

Counselors, social workers, and support programs can help people with Hodgkin's disease deal with their emotions. Family and friends can be a source of strength, too.

People who have been successfully treated for Hodgkin's disease must follow up with regular doctor appointments and medical tests.

A serious illness such as Hodgkin's disease can cause people to change their values and goals.

Chapter 5

Brian's Story

Brian is a high school junior who has been battling Hodgkin's disease for the past year. It's been a rough experience.

A Strange Lump
One evening last February, Brian and his girlfriend, Corey, were watching television at Brian's house. Brian asked Corey to give him a backrub. As Corey's hands moved across Brian's right shoulder, she noticed a lump about the size of a quarter. "Hey, you've got some kind of lump here," she said. "You'd better get it checked out."

Brian Gets Bad News

Brian's mom took him to the family doctor. Dr. Williams was casual about the lump but wanted it removed and examined. At school on the day after his surgery, Brian showed off the scar on his shoulder where the lump had been. Some kids thought it looked cool, but others said it was gross.

When Brian arrived home from school that day, he was surprised to see his mom's car in the driveway. She usually didn't get home from work until later. The minute he got in the house, she sat down with him on the sofa. She explained that the tests on the lump had come back. They showed that Brian had something called Hodgkin's disease, a form of cancer. It was serious.

An hour later, Brian and his mom and dad were sitting in the oncologist's office. Dr. Martinez explained that Hodgkin's disease is a cancer that strikes the lymphatic system. She told them that it affects the body's ability to defend itself against diseases and infections. Dr. Martinez also said that Brian's chance of survival was pretty good. More than 90 percent of people Brian's age can be cured with radiation, chemotherapy, or a combination of both.

Hodgkin's Disease

Brian and his parents had lots of questions during his treatment. Here are a few good ones to ask:

- What kind of Hodgkin's disease do I have?
- What stage of Hodgkin's disease is it?
- What are the treatment choices?
- What should I do to be ready for treatment?
- Is it okay to go back to school?

"I didn't hear a word the doctor said. I didn't even think about this horrible disease that I could die from. Instead, I was worried about what I was supposed to do about school, my grades, basketball. I worried about losing my hair from chemo and what Corey would think. I didn't want to be sick!"

Brian Says:

Brian's Chemotherapy

Brian began chemotherapy treatment two weeks later. He took a mix of drugs called ABVD. This mix contains the drugs adriamycin, bleomycin, vinblastine, and dacarbazine. Brian had his first treatment session in the hospital so doctors could monitor his body's reaction. After that, his mom drove him to the hospital's outpatient clinic. At each session, the mixture of highly toxic drugs was injected into his body. Brian said it was like getting poisoned.

Myth: People with cancer did something to cause their illness.

Fact: This may be true with some cancers. Smoking, for example, has been proven to cause lung cancer. Sunbathing can lead to skin cancer. In the case of Hodgkin's disease, however, no specific behavior is known to cause this illness.

> **Brian's Parents Say:**
>
> "At first, Brian was angry that Hodgkin's disease had happened to him. He'd say, 'This isn't fair. This isn't how my life was supposed to be.' Later on, he expressed feelings of guilt. He wondered what he had done to cause his illness, and he worried that he was causing the family so much trouble. We assured him that Hodgkin's disease had nothing to do with him as a person or what he deserved."

Brian's chemotherapy went on all spring. He'd have a week of intense chemo followed by two weeks off to give his body time to recover. Brian seldom felt well enough to go to school. He spent most of his time lying in bed and staring at the TV. Corey would come over to keep him company when he felt up to it. When Brian did go out, he wore long-sleeved shirts. These hid the purple bruises on his arms from the injections and IVs. The chemotherapy killed Brian's healthy blood cells. So he had difficulty fighting infection and often had to be in the hospital.

"We were all scared, but it helped to talk about our feelings. Brian would ask, 'Am I going to die?' I'd say, 'No, at least not from Hodgkin's disease.'"
—Brian's mom

Brian Says:

"I had pain in my legs, back, and stomach. The nausea got worse and worse. I couldn't eat anything and lost about 30 pounds. I looked like a bald-headed bag of bones. It got so I dreaded going to chemo. My parents practically had to drag me there.

"About the only thing that got me through was knowing that my chances of a complete cure were high. That and talking to Damian, my 'chemo buddy.' Damian was a kid my age with leukemia. A social worker at the hospital introduced us. It helped to talk with someone who knew what I was going through."

Brian's Radiation Therapy

Brian finished his last chemo session at the end of June. As the drugs left his system, he felt well enough to spend weekends at a camp for kids with cancer. He couldn't hike up hills or swim very far, but it was still fun to be outdoors.

Brian believes that some good came from having Hodgkin's disease. He thinks the experience made him a stronger person.

Schoolwork came back into Brian's life. His parents hired a tutor to help him make up what he had missed. Corey helped him study, too. He took his exams and did well.

Brian's doctors wanted him to have radiation therapy as a safety measure. If any cancer cells remained, the powerful X rays should kill them. At the end of July, Brian began 12 courses of low-dose radiation. He joked that now he was getting burned. His dad drove him to the hospital for treatments. The worst side effect was very bad nausea. Brian kept a plastic ice cream bucket in the car. He knew that on the way home he would throw up.

Good News for Brian

By fall, life was returning to normal for Brian and his family. Tests after the chemo and radiation showed no traces of cancer in his body. His physical strength was returning slowly, and his hair, eyelashes, and eyebrows were growing back. Brian will continue to be tested regularly in the months and years to come. Because of the chemo and radiation, he has a slightly increased risk of developing other cancers. He also is at risk for heart disease and thyroid problems.

Hockey great Mario Lemieux was diagnosed with Hodgkin's disease in 1993. His diagnosis came one year after he first noticed a small lump in his neck. When he realized that the lump had started to grow, he talked with his team doctor. After 22 radiation treatments, Lemieux resumed playing for the Pittsburgh Penguins. He only played part of the 1993–1994 season. However, he still scored more goals than any other player did. He also was named the National Hockey League's Most Valuable Player.

Brian Says:

"It's strange to say, but I believe having Hodgkin's disease made me a stronger person. I think that if I can beat cancer, I can do anything. My values have changed, too. Like now, looking good and acting cool aren't so important. Keeping healthy is very important, and being with people I like is a big thing."

Points to Consider

Name some emotions a person with a serious illness might face. Why would the person have each emotion? Why is it important to deal with these emotions?

How might having a serious illness change your life?

What are some good and bad things that might result from having Hodgkin's disease as a teen?

Chapter Overview

Today, most people treated for Hodgkin's disease can look forward to a life free from this illness.

Scientists continue to look for the causes of Hodgkin's disease, as well as better ways to diagnose and treat it.

One promising new treatment is biological therapy, which uses the body's immune system to fight cancer. Monoclonal antibodies, cancer vaccines, and cytokines are examples of biological therapy.

Bone marrow transplants and stem cell transplants may become more common in treating people with Hodgkin's disease. Scientists are working to improve these procedures.

Chapter 6

Looking Ahead

Forty years ago, a diagnosis of Hodgkin's disease usually meant certain death for anyone who had it. Thanks to the efforts of scientists and doctors, this is no longer true. Most people with Hodgkin's disease now can look forward to a healthy life. In addition, researchers continue to find better ways of diagnosing and treating lymphomas. New discoveries may increase the chance of survival for all people with Hodgkin's disease.

Did You Know?

According to the 1959 edition of the *World Book Encyclopedia*, Hodgkin's disease "is fatal usually within a few years." A lot has happened over the years to reverse this statement. Today, Hodgkin's disease is one of the most treatable forms of cancer.

Biological Therapy

One promising new area of treatment is biological therapy, or immunotherapy. Biological therapy uses the body's immune system to seek and destroy cancer cells. The immune system is the body's natural ability to protect itself against disease. Some kinds of biological therapy are monoclonal antibodies, vaccines, and cytokines. These drug treatments currently are being tested or used on a limited basis.

Monoclonal Antibodies

Monoclonal antibodies are manufactured in a laboratory from a living parent cell. They are given intravenously. Monoclonal antibodies are called "smart drugs" because they target only cancer cells. By avoiding healthy cells, monoclonal antibodies produce fewer harmful side effects than other drugs do. They may kill cancer cells more quickly than chemotherapy or radiation therapy. This would reduce the amount of time a person must spend in treatment. The U.S. government recently approved two monoclonal antibodies for lymphoma treatment.

Promising new drugs must go through clinical trials before they can be approved for use by the public. Clinical trials are carefully controlled studies using actual people. Teens with Hodgkin's disease can participate in clinical trials with the consent of their parent or guardian. You can find out about current clinical trials by contacting the National Cancer Institute's Cancer Information Service. Call 1-800-4-CANCER (800-422-6237) or log on to the Internet at *cancertrials.nci.nih.gov*.

Cancer Vaccines

Vaccines are being developed that stimulate the immune system to destroy lymphoma cells. One kind of vaccine is manufactured in a laboratory using the person's own tumor cells. Cancer vaccines don't prevent a person from getting cancer. This makes these vaccines different from vaccines against measles, chicken pox, polio, and other diseases. Cancer vaccines are given after the person has been treated with chemotherapy or radiation and is in remission. Their purpose is to prevent a relapse, or return of the disease.

Cytokines

Cytokines are chemicals that occur naturally in the body. They stimulate the body to respond to disease. Scientists now can make cytokines in the laboratory. Two kinds of cytokines used in lymphoma treatment are interferons and interleukins. Another kind, called colony-stimulating factors, stimulates the production of blood cells. People need a supply of healthy blood cells to withstand high doses of chemotherapy. Cytokines are given by injections.

Scientists are looking for ways to make chemotherapy and radiation more tolerable. One chemotherapy treatment being tested has more drugs than current chemotherapy treatments. However, the amount of each drug is decreased. Using smaller amounts of more drugs may cause fewer side effects while delivering the same cancer-killing punch.

Bone Marrow Transplant

Bone marrow transplants may become more common in treating Hodgkin's disease. As mentioned before, bone marrow is the tissue inside bones that manufactures blood cells. Chemotherapy and radiation therapy destroy bone marrow. A successful bone marrow transplant restores blood cell production. Bone marrow transplants, along with high-dose chemotherapy, are being used to treat people with recurrent or resistant Hodgkin's disease.

There are two types of bone marrow transplants. One type uses marrow that has been taken from the person with Hodgkin's disease and stored. The marrow was collected at a time when the person was relatively free of cancer. The other type of bone marrow transplant uses marrow from a donor. The donor's marrow must be a genetic match for the person's marrow. A surgeon harvests the marrow with a hollow needle by withdrawing the marrow from the person or donor's hipbone.

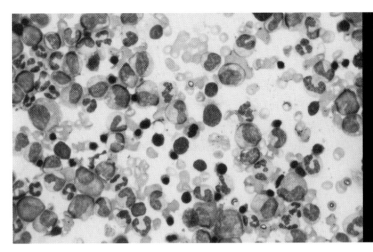

Before the transplant, the person is given the high-dose chemotherapy needed to kill the cancer cells. The person also may receive radiation therapy. The healthy marrow then is injected into the person's bloodstream. If all goes well, the transplanted marrow begins producing new blood cells in one or two weeks. Until this marrow begins to grow, the person must receive drugs and blood transfusions. This is to protect him or her from infection and bleeding. It also protects the person from anemia, which means having a low number of red blood cells.

A bone marrow transplant can be extremely painful and stressful. Scientists are searching for ways to improve the procedure. Finding donor marrow that matches the person's marrow can be very difficult. A way to use nonmatching marrow is needed. Researchers are trying to determine when bone marrow transplants are most effective. They're testing the difference between doing these transplants in earlier stages of Hodgkin's disease rather than later stages.

"After my first round of treatment for Hodgkin's disease, the doctors harvested and froze my bone marrow. They said it was like an insurance policy in case my Hodgkin's came back. Well, a year later it did come back stronger than ever, and I needed a bone marrow transplant.

Angie, Age 15

"I had to be in the hospital for five days before the transplant. The doctors gave me chemo that really made me sick. I just kept throwing up. It felt like an explosion had gone off inside me.

"On the day of the transplant, a nurse came into my room with the bags of frozen marrow. There were eight plastic bags in all, each with my name on it. One at a time, the nurse put each bag in warm water to thaw it. Then she filled a large syringe with the marrow and handed it to the doctor. The doctor injected the marrow into my bloodstream through a tube in my chest. It took 16 syringes to use up all the marrow.

"The doctor said the marrow would find its way to the bones. There it would grow and produce the blood cells I needed to live.

"I was in the hospital for a month after the transplant. The doctors gave me drugs to fight infection. I had a lot of complications, and it was a long time before I felt like eating anything. Finally, I felt strong enough to go home.

"So far, the transplant seems to be working. I need to be very careful about avoiding germs, though. I stay away from crowded places, like movie theaters, and I wash my hands a lot.

"I still have nightmares about having cancer. But I can go most of the day now without thinking about it. Maybe someday I'll reach a point where I don't think about cancer at all."

Today, Hodgkin's disease is a highly curable cancer. Better ways of treating and diagnosing the disease may further increase people's chances for survival.

Stem Cell Transplant

Another kind of transplant that may help people with Hodgkin's disease is stem cell transplant. A stem cell is an immature cell. A machine removes the person's blood a little at a time. It then takes out only the stem cells and returns the rest of the blood to the body. The harvested stem cells are frozen until they're returned to the person through a transplant. Researchers are discovering that these transplants may be better than bone marrow transplants in restoring blood cell production.

Points to Consider

What could you do to educate other people about Hodgkin's disease?

How could you help raise money for cancer research?

If you had Hodgkin's disease, would you volunteer to test a new drug? Why or why not?

Glossary

antibody (AN-ti-bod-ee)—a substance produced by lymphocytes to fight infection and disease

biopsy (BYE-op-see)—removal and examination of fluid and tissue from the living body; doctors perform biopsies to aid in diagnoses.

immune system (i-MYOON SISS-tuhm)—the group of organs and cells that defend the body against infection and disease; the lymph system is part of the immune system.

lymph (LIMF)—a colorless liquid that travels through the lymph system; lymph carries cells that fight infection.

lymphocyte (LIM-fuh-site)—a white blood cell; lymphocytes fight infection and disease.

lymphoma (lim-FOH-muh)—cancer of the lymph system

metastasize (muh-TASS-tuh-size)—to spread from one part of the body to another

mononucleosis (mon-oh-noo-klee-OH-siss)—a contagious disease that causes weakness and fatigue; "mono" tends to strike people in their late teens.

nausea (NAW-zee-uh)—upset stomach

oncologist (ahn-KAH-luh-jist)—a doctor who specializes in diagnosing and treating cancer

remission (ri-MISH-uhn)—a period when there are no active signs of a disease

resistance (ri-ZISS-tuhnss)—the ability to withstand something; people with Hodgkin's disease might develop resistance to treatment, which means the treatment no longer works.

spleen (SPLEEN)—an organ of the lymph system; the spleen is located on the left side of the abdomen near the stomach.

tumor (TOO-mur)—an abnormal lump or mass of cells; a tumor may be cancerous or noncancerous.

For More Information

Dorfman, Elena. *The C-Word: Teenagers and Their Families Living With Cancer.* Portland, OR: NewSage Press, 1994.

Gold, John Coopersmith. *Cancer.* Rev. ed. Berkeley Heights, NJ: Enslow, 2000.

Jordheim, Anne E. *What Every Young Person Should Know About Cancer.* Kettering, OH: PPI Publishing, 1996.

Tarcy, Brian. *Mario Lemieux: Ice Hockey Star.* New York: Chelsea House, 1995.

Yount, Lisa. *Cancer.* San Diego, CA: Lucent Books, 1999.

Note At publication, all resources listed here were accurate and appropriate to the topics covered in this book. Addresses and phone numbers may change. When visiting Internet sites and links, use good judgment. Remember, never give personal information over the Internet.

Useful Addresses and Internet Sites

American Cancer Society
1599 Clifton Road Northeast
Atlanta, GA 30329
1-800-ACS-2345 (800-227-2345)
www.cancer.org

Canadian Cancer Society
10 Alcorn Avenue, Suite 200
Toronto, ON M4V 3B1
CANADA
1-888-939-3333

The Leukemia and Lymphoma Society
1311 Mamaroneck Avenue
White Plains, NY 10605
1-800-955-4572
www.leukemia-lymphoma.org

Lymphoma Research Foundation of America
8800 Venice Boulevard, Suite 207
Los Angeles, CA 90034

Cancer Survivors Network
www.acscsn.org
Provides an online community offering
information and support

Candlelighters Childhood Cancer Foundation
www.candlelighters.org
Contains information, support, and
message boards

CureHodgkin's.com
www.curehodgkins.com
Contains resources for people with Hodgkin's
disease and their families

Guide to Internet Resources for Cancer:
The Hodgkin's Disease Page
www.cancerindex.org/clinks2i.htm
Provides links to organizations and web pages
on personal experience with Hodgkin's disease

Hodgkin's Disease Mail List
www.hodgkinsdisease.org
Provides an Internet mailing list for
information on Hodgkin's disease

KidsHealth
www.kidshealth.org
Has a teen section with plain-talk information
on many topics, including cancer and
Hodgkin's disease

Index

acupuncture, 31
alternative therapy, 31–32
antibiotics, 15, 16

biofeedback, 31
biological therapy, 54–55
biopsy, 14, 17–18, 21, 24
blood cells, white, 6–8, 27, 42, 57
blood tests, 16, 27, 38
bone marrow transplants, 31, 56–58
breath, shortness of, 14, 25

cancers, risks of developing other, 30, 50
Cell-Mates, 38
chemotherapy, 10, 23, 26–27, 36, 41, 47–49, 55, 56, 58
  high-dose, 55, 57
  long-term side effects of, 29–30, 38
  short-term side effects of, 27–28, 43
clinical trials, 55
colony-stimulating factors, 55
complementary therapy, 31, 32
computed tomography (CT) scan, 17, 20
computers, 17, 24, 43
coughing, 14, 25
cytokines, 54, 55

death, 8, 9–10, 53
diarrhea, 25
drugs, 26–27, 31–32, 47, 54–56, 58. *See also* chemotherapy

Epstein-Barr virus, 9
exercise, 37, 38, 51

feelings about Hodgkin's Disease, 35, 37, 39, 40, 41, 47–48
fertility loss, 30
fevers, 14, 16

gallium scans, 20

hair loss, 27, 28, 36, 41, 47
Hodgkin, Thomas, 5
Hodgkin's Disease
  causes of, 9
  coping with, 35–43
  diagnosing, 13–21, 53
  helping a family member or friend through, 39–43
  risk factors for, 10–11
  treatment for, 23–33, 53, 54–59
  types of, 19–21, 47
  what is it?, 5–11
  who gets it?, 10
hypothyroidism, 30

imaging tests, 16–17, 38
immune system, 6, 10, 30, 54
immunotherapy. *See* biological therapy
infections, 15, 27, 30, 38, 42, 46, 48, 58
interferons, 55
interleukins, 55
intravenous (IV) infusion, 26–27, 54
itching, 14, 16, 25, 31

late effects, 30, 38
learning problems, 30
Lemieux, Mario, 51
lumps, 13, 45–46
lymph nodes, 6, 8–9, 13, 15, 18, 20
lymph system, 5, 6–7, 46
lymphocyte depleted, 19
lymphocyte predominant, 19
lymphocytes, 6–8, 13
lymphomas, 5, 7–9, 30, 38, 55
    non-Hodgkin's, 8–9

magnetic resonance imaging (MRI),
    17, 20
medical history, 14, 15
medical tests, 14, 15, 16–17, 20–21
mixed cellularity, 19
monoclonal antibodies, 54
mononucleosis, 9, 10, 13, 16
myths, 48

nausea, 14, 25, 27, 31, 49, 50
night sweats, 14, 16, 20
nodular sclerosis, 19
nutrition, 37, 38

oncologists, 26, 37, 46

pain, physical, 8, 14, 21, 23, 31, 37,
    49
pathologists, 18
physical exams, 14, 15, 38, 46
platelets, 27

radiation therapy, 23–27, 36, 56, 57
    in children and teens, 26, 49–51
    external beam, 24–25
    long-term side effects of, 29–30,
        38
    short-term side effects of, 25, 50
recurrence, 31, 56, 58
Reed-Sternberg (R-S) cells, 8, 18
remission, 29, 31, 41

school, 25, 42–43, 47, 50
screening tests, 19
spleen, 7, 17, 20
staging, 19–21, 47
stem cell transplant, 59
stress management, 31, 38
support groups, 37, 38, 49
symptoms, 13–14, 20–21, 45

talking, 38, 40, 41, 42, 49
thymus, 7
tiredness, 14, 25, 27
tonsils, 7
tuberculosis, 13
tumors, 5, 7–8, 14, 17, 18, 20–21, 23

urinary problems, 25, 43

vaccines, 54, 55
viruses, 9
vomiting, 14, 25, 27, 31, 50, 58

weakness, 9, 25, 27
weight loss, 9, 14, 49

X rays, 17, 20, 21, 23